What Does a Cow Say?

Seed Learning

COW

duck

turkey

sheep

chick

donkey

kitten

rooster

What does a cow say?

A cow says, "Mooooooooooooo!"

What does a duck say?

A duck says, "Quack! Quack! Quack!"

What does a sheep say?

A sheep says,
"Baaaaaaaaaaaaaaaa!

What does a turkey say?

A turkey says, "Gobble! Gobble! Gobble!"

What does
a donkey say?

A donkey says,
"Hee-haw! Hee-haw!"

What does
a rooster say?

A rooster says,
Cock-a-doodle-doo!"

Let's learn more about New Zealand.

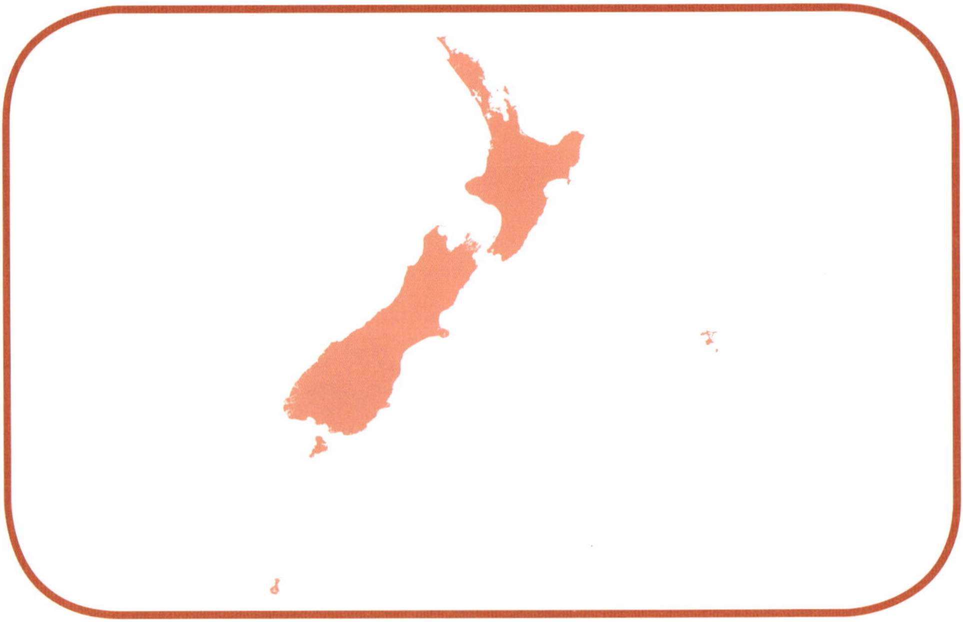

Maori Hangi